Vegan Smoothie Recipes

The Delicious, Weight Loss
& Healthy Living Vegan
Smoothie Recipe Book

Table of Contents

Why Go Vegan?

Veganism (also called Plant Based Eating), is a diet that includes fresh fruit, vegetables, grains, nuts and seeds. A well rounded Vegan diet includes many vitamins and nutrients that support body function.

A major contributing factor to people becoming Vegan is concern over the way farm animals are treated. Vegans believe that including animal products in our diets is unnecessary. Vegans feel the cruelty and treatment of animals is unacceptable, and they live their lives in support of humane and compassionate treatment of all living creatures.

In addition, studies have shown that eating a Vegan diet can provide numerous benefits, including:

- **It's Super Good For You!**

  Eating Vegan is great for your health! Studies show that eating a diet high in fruits, vegetables, nuts and seeds decreases your chance of developing diseases like diabetes, heart disease, high blood pressure and more. The Vegan diet includes numerous vitamins, minerals, plant protein and fiber that will keep you going strong!

- **You Can Normalize Your Weight!**

  It goes without saying that if you include mainly fruits and vegetables in your diet, you probably won't have weight issues. Vegans on average weigh about 20 pounds less than meat eaters. They also sustain their weight over a longer period of time due to the diet being a lifestyle change, rather than some fad that isn't good for you and doesn't keep the weight off.

- **Longer Lifespan?**

  In some parts of the world, age is a minor factor in the quality of life they lead. This is due to the fact that they eat little or no processed foods, eat very little meat, and stay active even in their later years. Eating Vegan will not only help you to live longer because of the nutrients your body will get, it will help you live a better quality of life as you age.

- **Eating Vegan is Tasty!**

Yes, you'll have to give up things like hamburgers, ice-cream and fried chicken; however, as the demand for Vegan eating grows, so do the great alternatives that taste like these foods, but without the unhealthy side effects. Smoothies are a great way to get your daily serving of fruits, vegetables, nuts and seeds in an easy and delicious way!

Smoothie Basics

I use a variety of ingredients for my smoothies and shakes to make them Vegan. Most are pretty standard; however, you may have to find some things at a health store, rather than a regular grocery store. Here's a breakdown of some of the ingredients I use and tips for creating the best smoothie ever:

- **Vegan Milk**

  There are a wide variety of Vegan milk substitutes. These include almond milk, soy milk, rice milk, coconut milk, and hemp milk, among others. Any recipe that calls for milk can also be replaced with plain water or fruit juice.

- **Ice Cream**

  The same is true for ice cream substitutes. You can use coconut ice cream or soy ice cream. These are available at most major grocery stores or at stores like Whole Foods.

- **Whipped Coconut Cream**

  If you are making a dessert shake, you can make coconut whipped cream. You must use full-fat coconut milk or coconut cream. Some brands work better than others. Chill the can for at least 24 hours before whipping. Flip the can upside down and pour off the liquid. This liquid can be used as a milk substitute. Scoop the hard solids at the bottom into a bowl and whip until thickened. Add a teaspoon of vanilla extract and a tablespoon of sweetener to the cream. It will keep for up to one week in the refrigerator.

- **Frozen Watermelon & Other Fruit**

  Frozen watermelon cubes are used to give shakes a more icy consistency. To make, cut a watermelon into 1" cubes and place on a baking sheet. Freeze for at least 3 hours before using. Other fruits can have the same effect and help smoothies and shakes have a thick and cold consistency. Of course, you don't need to freeze your fruit at all if you want a thinner drink. I use a lot of frozen bananas because they whip up thick and delicious, but freezing is completely optional.

- **Sweeteners**

  I mainly use pure maple syrup or agave nectar in my smoothies and shakes. However; you can use the following alternative sugar substitutes as well. These are healthier than refined white sugar:

  Sucanut: An all-natural brown sugar alternative found in health stores.

  Evaporated Cane Juice: Crystallized cane juice that is a healthier alternative to white sugar.

  Coconut Sugar: A sugar made from sap in the flower of a coconut palm plant. It retains minerals and nutrients missing from regular white sugar.

- **Extra Flavor**

  If your drink tastes bland, try adding a pinch of salt, a squeeze of lemon (especially for fruity drinks), or a little extra sweetener. Since fruit sweetness can vary by time of the year, you may need a little extra flavor boost.

- **Ice**

I use ice in most of my smoothies and shakes because I like the slushy, icy texture and I love it ice cold! However, you can easily omit this and still have a delicious drink.

Delicious Vegan Smoothies & Shakes

One of my favorite things to do is throw a bunch of healthy ingredients into a high speed blender! It is so easy to get your daily serving of fruits and vegetables this way. And not only is it nutritious, it's incredibly delicious!

Peanut Butter Chocolate Shake

Chocolate and peanut butter combine for a sure favorite!

Serves 1

Ingredients

  1 cup vanilla coconut ice cream
  2 Tbsp. cocoa powder
  2 Tbsp. peanut butter
  ¼ cup non-dairy milk
  1 frozen banana
  A few ice cubes

Instructions

Combine all ingredients in blender. Puree until smooth. Add water or non-dairy milk to thin shake if consistency is too thick.

Emma's Matcha Shake

Matcha tea is a highly nutritional green tea from Japan. It is full of antioxidants, fiber and chlorophyll, which makes it one of my favorite ingredients for shakes and smoothies!

Serves 1

Ingredients

> 3/4 cup non-dairy milk
> 1 cup frozen watermelon cubes
> 1 frozen banana
> 1 tsp. matcha green tea powder
> 1 tsp. chia seeds

Instructions

Combine all ingredients in blender. Puree until smooth. Add water or non-dairy milk to thin shake if consistency is too thick.

Cashew Strawberry Smoothie

This is a very satisfying smoothie that is perfect for breakfast or when you want a healthy snack!

Serves 1

Ingredients

1 cup vanilla non-dairy milk
½ cup frozen strawberries
½ cup frozen watermelon cubes
1 banana, frozen
1 Tbsp. creamy cashew butter
Pinch of sea salt

Instructions

Combine all ingredients in blender. Puree until smooth. Add water or non-dairy milk to thin shake if consistency is too thick.

Watermelon Vanilla Smoothie

Besides being incredibly delicious, vanilla bean has been shown to increase mental performance!

Serves 1

Ingredients

1 cup frozen watermelon cubes
1 frozen banana
½ cup vanilla non-dairy milk
1 Tbsp. vanilla protein powder
1 tsp. vanilla extract
Seeds from 1 vanilla bean

Instructions

Combine all ingredients in blender. Puree until smooth. Add water or non-dairy milk to thin shake if consistency is too thick.

Wild Blueberry Shake

What could be better than the delicious taste of blueberries – never mind the fact that they are chock-full of antioxidants and provide rich amounts of vitamin C!

Serves 1

Ingredients

> 1 cup wild blueberries
> 1 frozen banana
> ½ cup vanilla non-dairy milk
> 1 Tbsp. vanilla protein powder
> A few ice cubes

Instruction

Combine all ingredients in blender. Puree until smooth. Add water or non-dairy milk to thin shake if consistency is too thick.

Chocolate Covered Strawberry Shake

Chocolaty, strawberry goodness – yum!

Serves 1

Ingredients

- 1 frozen banana
- 1 cup frozen strawberries
- ½ cup non-dairy milk
- ¼ cup hazelnuts
- 2 Tbsp. pure maple syrup
- 2 Tbsp. cocoa powder
- 1 tsp. vanilla extract
- 1 ½ cups ice

Instructions

Combine all ingredients in blender. Puree until smooth. Add water or non-dairy milk to thin shake if consistency is too thick.

Almond Butter Spice Shake

The spice in this recipe gives an extra kick that is deliciously different!

Serves 1

Ingredients

  1 cup non-dairy milk
  2 frozen bananas
  2 Tbsp. creamy almond butter
  ½ tsp. ginger powder
  ¼ tsp. cinnamon
  Dash of cayenne
  Dash of nutmeg
  ¼ cup chopped almonds

Instructions

Combine all ingredients except almonds in blender. Puree until smooth. Add water or non-dairy milk to thin shake if consistency is too thick. Garnish with chopped almonds.

Double Chocolate Chip Shake

This shake satisfies those chocolate cravings!

Serves 1

Ingredients

1 cup non-dairy chocolate ice cream
1 cup non-dairy chocolate milk
¼ cup chocolate chips
½ frozen banana
2 Tbsp. cocoa powder
1 Tbsp. peanut butter
1 tsp. ground cinnamon
¼ tsp. sea salt
Dash of cayenne pepper
A few ice cubes

Instructions

Combine all ingredients in blender. Puree until smooth. Add water or non-dairy milk to thin shake if consistency is too thick.

Calming Chamomile Banana Smoothie

This is a great after dinner smoothie – the chamomile tea is a nice addition!

Serves 1

Ingredients

¼ cup non-dairy milk
¼ cup brewed chamomile tea
¼ cup raw cashews
2 frozen bananas
1 tsp. ground cinnamon
1 tsp. maple syrup
A few ice cubes

Instructions

Combine all ingredients in blender. Puree until smooth. Add water or non-dairy milk to thin shake if consistency is too thick.

Frozen S'mores Shake

This shake will make you feel like a kid with its fun flavors!

Serves 1

Ingredients

- 1 cup non-dairy ice cream
- 1 cup vanilla non-dairy milk
- 1 frozen banana
- 2 Tbsp. cocoa powder
- 1 tsp. ground cinnamon
- A few ice cubes
- Vegan mini-marshmallows
- Crushed graham crackers

Instructions

Combine all ingredients except for marshmallows and graham cracker crumbs in blender. Puree until smooth. Add water or non-dairy milk to thin shake if consistency is too thick. Garnish with marshmallows and graham crackers.

Spiced Black Currant Smoothie

A dark, rich & full of antioxidants smoothie!

Serves 1

Ingredients

> 1 cup black currant juice
> 1 cup frozen blueberries
> ½ cup ice cubes
> ½ cup non-dairy yogurt
> ¼ tsp. of cayenne
> ¼ tsp. vanilla extract
> ¼ tsp. ground cinnamon

Instructions

Combine all ingredients in blender. Puree until smooth. Add water or non-dairy milk to thin shake if consistency is too thick.

Coconut Chai Shake

Chai is one of my favorite flavors and this shake always hits the spot!

Serves 2

Ingredients

    5 Medjool dates
    2 frozen bananas
    ½ cup chai concentrate
    ¼ cup non-dairy milk
    1 cup ice cubes
    ½ tsp. ground cinnamon
    ½ tsp. ground ginger

Instructions

Combine all ingredients in blender. Puree until smooth. Add water or non-dairy milk to thin shake if consistency is too thick.

Apple Pie Smoothie

Apples & spices collide to create a wonderful smoothie!

Serves 1

Ingredients

1 apple
½ cup frozen apple juice concentrate
1 cup vanilla non-dairy yogurt
1 ½ tsp. pumpkin pie spice
1 cup water
A few ice cubes

Instructions

Combine all ingredients in blender. Puree until smooth. Add water or non-dairy milk to thin shake if consistency is too thick.

North Pole Shake

The candy canes give this shake a festive and fun touch!

Serves 2

Ingredients

 1 cup vanilla non-dairy ice cream
 1 cup non-dairy milk
 1 cup frozen strawberries
 1 frozen banana
 1 cup ice cubes
 ¼ cup chocolate chips
 2 Tbsp. crushed candy canes

Instructions

Combine all ingredients except for candy canes in blender. Puree until smooth. Add water or non-dairy milk to thin shake if consistency is too thick. Sprinkle candy canes on top of smoothie.

Citrus Avocado Smoothie

Avocados are full of fiber, healthy fats, protein, vitamins & minerals!

Serves 1

Ingredients

1 avocado, pitted
1 frozen banana
½ cup orange juice
Juice and zest of 1 lime
1 cup coconut milk
Pinch of sea salt
A few ice cubes

Instructions

Combine all ingredients in blender. Puree until smooth. Add water or non-dairy milk to thin shake if consistency is too thick.

Green Monster Smoothie

Get your daily serving of greens with this delicious smoothie!

Serves 1

Ingredients

    1 large orange, peeled
    1 cup kale
    1 cup baby spinach leaves
    ¼ cup parsley
    ½ avocado, pitted
    1 apple, chopped
    1 cup coconut water
    1 Tbsp. lemon juice
    Dash cayenne pepper
    A few ice cubes

Instructions

Combine all ingredients in blender. Puree until smooth. Add water or non-dairy milk to thin shake if consistency is too thick.

Sunshine Smoothie

This smoothie gives you a good dose of vitamin C!

Serves 1

Ingredients

> 1 cup Swiss chard
> 1 large orange, peeled
> ½ cup grapefruit juice
> ½ cup frozen grapes
> ½ frozen banana
> 1 cup water
> A few ice cubes

Instructions

Combine all ingredients in blender. Puree until smooth. Add water or non-dairy milk to thin shake if consistency is too thick.

Spinach Raspberry Shake

A lovely mixture of flavors makes this shake truly special!

Serves 1

Ingredients

  2 cups spinach
  1 cup frozen raspberries
  1 cup non-dairy milk
  2 Tbsp. ground flaxseed
  2 Tbsp. shredded coconut
  1 Tbsp. hazelnut butter
  A few ice cubes

Instructions

Combine all ingredients in blender. Puree until smooth. Add water or non-dairy milk to thin shake if consistency is too thick.

Mom's Banana Bread Shake

Your mom's banana bread in a healthy, yummy shake!

Serves 1

Ingredients

>   1 cup water
>   2 frozen bananas
>   1/3 cup cooked and cooled quinoa
>   2 medjool dates, pitted
>   1 Tbsp. chopped walnuts
>   2 tsp. flax oil
>   1 tsp. vanilla extract
>   1 tsp. ground cinnamon

Instructions

Combine all ingredients in blender. Puree until smooth. Add water or non-dairy milk to thin shake if consistency is too thick.

Strawberry Cheesecake Smoothie

Strawberries are low in calories, high in fiber, and have nutritional properties that are good for bone, heart and eye health!

Serves 1

Ingredients

1 cup strawberries
1 cup non-dairy milk
3 Tbsp. oats
1 Tbsp. agave nectar
1 Tbsp. chia seed
1 Tbsp. chopped cashews
1 tsp. apple cider vinegar
1 tsp. lemon juice
½ tsp. vanilla
A few ice cubes

Instructions

Combine all ingredients in blender. Puree until smooth. Add water or non-dairy milk to thin shake if consistency is too thick.

Minty Chocolate Chip Shake

This is a perfect smoothie for a hot summer day!

Serves 1

Ingredients

½ cup brewed and cooled peppermint tea
½ cup non-dairy milk
2 cups spinach
1 frozen banana
3 Tbsp. chocolate chips
2 Tbsp. hemp hearts
1-2 drops food grade mint essential oil
A few ice cubes

Instructions

Combine all ingredients in blender. Puree until smooth. Add water or non-dairy milk to thin shake if consistency is too thick.

Blushing Apple Smoothie

Cherries provide you with plenty of fiber and potassium, which is helpful in keeping blood pressure low!

Serves 1

Ingredients

1 apple
½ cup pitted fresh cherries
½ cup fresh raspberries
½ medium cucumber
1 Tbsp. chia seed
½ cup water
A few ice cubes

Instructions

Combine all ingredients in blender. Puree until smooth. Add water or non-dairy milk to thin shake if consistency is too thick.

Raspberry Lemon Poppy-Seed Smoothie

This smoothie is a twist on a delicious dressing I make for my salads. I thought, "Why not try it in a smoothie?" I'm glad I did!

Serves 1

Ingredients

1 cup non-dairy milk
½ cup raspberries
2 Tbsp. oats
1 Tbsp. pure maple syrup
1 Tbsp. lemon juice
1 Tbsp. almond butter
1 Tbsp. chia seeds
1 tsp. poppy seeds
1 tsp. pure vanilla extract
½ tsp. lemon zest
A few ice cubes

Instructions

Combine all ingredients in blender. Puree until smooth. Add water or non-dairy milk to thin shake if consistency is too thick.

Strawberry-Banana Tea Smoothie

You'll love this smoothie with the traditional strawberry-banana flavors, but with the added nutritional benefit of green tea!

Serves 1

Ingredients

   1 frozen banana
   6 frozen strawberries
   1 cup brewed and cooled green tea
   1 scoop vanilla protein powder
   1 Tbsp. chia seeds

Instructions

Combine all ingredients in blender. Puree until smooth. Add water or non-dairy milk to thin shake if consistency is too thick.

Peachy Blueberry Shake

Peaches are a great way to get your vitamins A & C, and are helpful for good kidney health!

Serves 1

Ingredients

    1 peach
    1 cup blueberries
    1 cup vanilla soy milk
    1 Tbsp. ground flaxseed
    1 Tbsp. unsweetened shredded coconut
    A few ice cubes

Instructions

Combine all ingredients in blender. Puree until smooth. Add water or non-dairy milk to thin shake if consistency is too thick.

Pumpkin Spice Smoothie

Who doesn't love pumpkin pie flavors? That's what this festive smoothie is all about!

Serves 1

Ingredients

  1 cup non-dairy milk
  ½ cup canned pumpkin
  ½ frozen banana
  2 Tbsp. chopped pecan
  1 Tbsp. raisins
  1 Tbsp. pure maple syrup
  ½ tsp. vanilla extract
  ½ tsp. ground cinnamon
  1/8 tsp. ground ginger
  1/8 tsp. ground nutmeg
  1/8 tsp. ground cloves
  1/8 tsp. all spice
  A few ice cubes

Instructions

Combine all ingredients in blender. Puree until smooth. Add water or non-dairy milk to thin shake if consistency is too thick.

Classic Green Smoothie

A perfect way to eat your greens!

Serves 1

Ingredients

 2 cups spinach
 1 cup kale
 1 cup almond milk
 1 medium apple, cored
 2 Tbsp. ground flaxseed
 1 Tbsp. almond butter
 A few ice cubes

Instructions

Combine all ingredients in blender. Puree until smooth. Add water or non-dairy milk to thin shake if consistency is too thick.

Caramel Apple Shake

Who knew caramel apples could be so good for you?!

Serves 1

Ingredients

1 cup non-dairy milk
1 apple
2 Tbsp. almond butter
2 cups spinach
2 medjool dates, pitted
½ tsp. pure vanilla extract
1/8 tsp. ground cinnamon
1/8 tsp. sea salt

Instructions

Combine all ingredients in blender. Puree until smooth. Add water or non-dairy milk to thin shake if consistency is too thick.

Key Lime Pie Smoothie

This smoothie will take you to the tropics with its light and refreshing flavors!

Serves 1

Ingredients

> 2 cups baby spinach leaves
> 1 cup non-dairy milk
> 1 frozen banana
> 1 Tbsp. agave nectar
> 1 Tbsp. sunflower butter
> 2 Tbsp. key lime juice
> 1 tsp. key lime zest
> ¼ tsp. pure vanilla extract
> A few ice cubes
> Crushed graham cracker and whipped coconut cream (for garnish)

Instructions

Combine all ingredients except for garnish in blender. Puree until smooth. Add water or non-dairy milk to thin shake if consistency is too thick. Garnish with graham cracker pieces or whipped coconut cream if desired.

Cinnamon Butternut Squash Shake

Butternut squash is rich in fiber, vitamin A & vitamin B6!

Serves 1

Ingredients

- 1 cup non-dairy milk
- 1 cup roasted and cooled butternut squash
- 4 Medjool dates, pitted
- 1 Tbsp. chia seeds
- 1 Tbsp. grated fresh ginger
- 2 tsp. ground cinnamon
- 1 tsp. vanilla extract

Instructions

Combine all ingredients in blender. Puree until smooth. Add water or non-dairy milk to thin shake if consistency is too thick.

Pink Power Smoothie

The coconut water in this recipe is very good for hydration, making this smoothie a great addition to hot summer days!

Serves 1

Ingredients

1 pear
½ avocado, pitted
1 cup frozen strawberries
1 beet, roughly chopped
1 cup frozen raspberries
1 cup coconut water
½ cup apple juice
Juice and zest from 1 lemon
A few ice cubes

Instructions

Combine all ingredients in blender. Puree until smooth. Add water or non-dairy milk to thin shake if consistency is too thick.

Raspberry Lime Smoothie

Raspberries and lime… ahh, heaven!

Serves 1

Ingredients

1 cup water
1 cup frozen raspberries
1 frozen banana
2 Tbsp. fresh lime juice
½ cup orange juice
2 tsp. agave nectar
A few ice cubes

Instructions

Combine all ingredients in blender. Puree until
smooth. Add water or non-dairy milk to thin shake
if consistency is too thick.

Chocolate Cake Batter Smoothie

This delicious smoothie is surprisingly similar to cake batter; yet, you'll find none of the unhealthy ingredients here!

Serves 1

Ingredients

1 ½ cups non-dairy milk
1/3 cups oats
1 frozen banana
1 Tbsp. cocoa powder
1 Tbsp. cashew butter
1 Tbsp. chocolate chips
1 tsp. ground cinnamon
1 tsp. vanilla
A few ice cubes

Instructions

Combine all ingredients in blender. Puree until smooth. Add water or non-dairy milk to thin shake if consistency is too thick.

Avocado "Eggnog" Smoothie

Traditional eggnog flavors combine in a nutritious, Vegan alternative to the sugary and high fat original!

Serves 1

Ingredients

1 cup full-fat coconut milk, chilled
1 cup non-dairy milk
¼ cup Bourbon (optional)
½ avocado, pitted
1 frozen banana
3 Tbsp. pure maple syrup
1 Tbsp. fresh lemon juice
1 tsp. vanilla extract
1 tsp. ground nutmeg
¼ tsp. ground cinnamon
1/8 tsp. ground cloves
A few ice cubes

Instructions

Combine all ingredients in blender. Puree until smooth. Add water or non-dairy milk to thin shake if consistency is too thick.

Pomegranate Apple Smoothie

Pomegranates are super good for your heart, and have a high antioxidant count that may help reduce the risk of disease!

Serves 1

Ingredients

> 1 cup pomegranate seeds
> 1 apple
> 1 cup strawberries
> 2 peeled kiwis
> 1 frozen banana
> 1 cup coconut water
> 1 Tbsp. ground flaxseed
> A few ice cubes

Instructions

Combine all ingredients in blender. Puree until smooth. Add water or non-dairy milk to thin shake if consistency is too thick.

Cucumber Pear Smoothie

A light and delicious smoothie that's perfect for breakfast or anytime!

Serves 1

Ingredients

- ½ cucumber, peeled
- 1 pear, chopped
- 1 cup non-dairy milk
- 1 Tbsp. almond butter
- 1 Tbsp. chia seeds
- 1 tsp. ground cinnamon
- A few ice cubes

Instructions

Combine all ingredients in blender. Puree until smooth. Add water or non-dairy milk to thin shake if consistency is too thick.

Avocado Tomato Basil Smoothie

Tomatoes are a good source of lycopene, which has been shown in studies to reduce the risk of certain types of cancer!

Serves 1

Ingredients

1 avocado, pitted
1 medium tomato
1 cucumber, peeled
½ cup fresh basil
1 ½ cups water
Juice of 1 lemon
1 Tbsp. agave nectar
A few ice cubes

Instructions

1. Combine all ingredients in blender. Puree until smooth. Add water or non-dairy milk to thin shake if consistency is too thick.

Red Velvet Shake

Beets are high in numerous vitamins and minerals, and they help to cleanse the liver and blood!

Serves 1

Ingredients

- 1 cup coconut milk
- 2 Tbsp. cocoa powder
- 2 Tbsp. chia seeds
- 1 medium beet, chopped
- 1 cup raspberries
- 1 cup strawberries
- A few ice cubes

Instructions

Combine all ingredients in blender. Puree until smooth. Add water or non-dairy milk to thin shake if consistency is too thick.

Orange Cherry Shake

A yummy mixture of healthy ingredients!

Serves 6

Ingredients

  1 frozen banana
  1 orange, peeled
  ½ cup cherries, pitted
  ½ cup watermelon cubes
  1 cup water
  A few ice cubes

Instructions

Combine all ingredients in blender. Puree until smooth. Add water or non-dairy milk to thin shake if consistency is too thick.

Cinnamon Pear Smoothie

Numerous studies have shown that cinnamon helps regulate blood sugar, and is high in calcium, iron and manganese!

Serves 1

Ingredients

    2 asian pears, chopped
    2 frozen bananas
    1 cup non-dairy milk
    1 tsp. ground cinnamon

Instructions

Combine all ingredients in blender. Puree until smooth. Add water or non-dairy milk to thin shake if consistency is too thick.

Basil Blackberry Smoothie

As a kid, I remember picking blackberries off our small patch in the back yard. What a treat it was to eat those juicy berries. I didn't realize how good they were for me until much later!

Serves 1

Ingredients

>1 cup frozen blackberries
>1 avocado, pitted
>1 cup non-dairy milk
>½ cup basil leaves
>1 tsp. vanilla extract
>A few ice cubes

Instructions

Combine all ingredients in blender. Puree until smooth. Add water or non-dairy milk to thin shake if consistency is too thick.

Vegan Pina Colada Shake

Pina colada is one of my absolute favorites!

Serves 1

Ingredients

    2 cups chopped pineapple
    1 cup full fat coconut milk
    1 frozen banana
    2 Tbsp. unsweetened shredded coconut
    1 Tbsp. agave nectar
    1 cup ice

Instructions

Combine all ingredients in blender. Puree until smooth. Add water or non-dairy milk to thin shake if consistency is too thick.

Mint & Kiwi Smoothie

Kiwis have naturally occurring enzymes that aid in digestion!

Serves 1

Ingredients

1 cup non-dairy milk
3 kiwis, peeled
1 cup baby spinach
1 frozen banana
¼ cup mint leaves
Juice and zest of 1 lime

Instructions

Combine all ingredients in blender. Puree until smooth. Add water or non-dairy milk to thin shake if consistency is too thick.

Black & Blue Smoothie

I love this smoothie packed with health-boosting antioxidants!

Serves 1

Ingredients

2 cups Swiss chard
1 cup frozen blackberries
1 cup frozen blueberries
1 frozen banana
1 Tbsp. grated fresh ginger
1 cup water
A few ice cubes

Instructions

Combine all ingredients in blender. Puree until smooth. Add water or non-dairy milk to thin shake if consistency is too thick.

Sweet Potato Festive Smoothie

This smoothie is fancy enough to serve to guests!

Serves 1

Ingredients

> 1 orange, peeled
> 1 sweet potato, cooked and cooled
> 1 medium apple
> 1/3 cup red grapes
> ¼ cup frozen cranberries
> 2 Medjool dates, pitted
> 1 Tbsp. fresh grated ginger
> 1 cup water
> A few ice cubes

Instructions

Combine all ingredients in blender. Puree until smooth. Add water or non-dairy milk to thin shake if consistency is too thick.

Lemon Cheesecake Smoothie

Cheesecake is hard to say "no" to, but you won't have to with this great-for-you alternative!

Serves 1

Ingredients

1 cup almond milk
2 Medjool dates, pitted
¼ cup raw cashews
Juice and zest of 2 lemons
1 frozen banana
1 Tbsp. pure maple syrup
1 tsp. lemon extract
1 tsp. vanilla extract
½ tsp. sea salt
A few ice cubes

Instructions

Combine all ingredients in blender. Puree until smooth. Add water or non-dairy milk to thin shake if consistency is too thick.

Raspberry Float Smoothie

This smoothie is great for kids – they think they're getting a real treat, but you know it's good for them!

Serves 1

Ingredients

2 cups frozen raspberries
4 Medjool dates, pitted
1 cup water
1 cup non-dairy ice cream
A few ice cubes
2 cups sparkling water (optional)

Instructions

Combine rapsberries, dates, water, ice cream and ice in blender. Puree until smooth.

Note: Mix with sparkling water to create a raspberry soda.

Rosemary Lemonade Smoothie

Rosemary is a woody herb that helps prevent disease, and is good for your brain and memory!

Serves 1

Ingredients

- 2 cups Romaine lettuce
- 2 cups watermelon cubes
- 1 cup coconut water
- 1 cucumber, peeled
- 1 Tbsp. chopped fresh rosemary
- Juice and zest of 1 lemon
- 2 tsp. agave nectar
- ½ tsp. salt

Instructions

Combine all ingredients in blender. Puree until smooth. Add water or non-dairy milk to thin shake if consistency is too thick.

Pineapple Dandelion Smoothie

Dandelion greens are great for cleansing and detoxing the body!

Serves 1

Ingredients

> 2 cups chopped pineapple
> 1 cup chopped dandelion greens
> 1 cup coconut water
> ¼ cup unsweetened shredded coconut
> ¼ cup raw cashews
> 2 Medjool dates, pitted
> A few ice cubes

Instructions

Combine all ingredients in blender. Puree until smooth. Add water or non-dairy milk to thin shake if consistency is too thick.

Cranberry Spice Shake

I love cranberries and this shake is the perfect way to enjoy them!

Serves 1

Ingredients

1 cup cranberries
1 avocado, pitted
1 small beet, chopped
1 cup water
¼ cup almonds
2 Tbsp. agave nectar
1 Tbsp. grated fresh ginger
Juice and zest of 1 lemon
1 tsp. ground cinnamon
A few ice cubes

Instructions

Combine all ingredients in blender. Puree until smooth. Add water or non-dairy milk to thin shake if consistency is too thick.

Mango Peachy Shake

Mangoes are high in vitamins A & C!

Serves 1

Ingredients

  1 mango, pitted
  1 large peach, pitted
  1 cup non-dairy milk
  1 Tbsp. chia seeds
  1 Tbsp. grated fresh ginger
  ½ tsp. ground cinnamon
  A few ice cubes

Instructions

Combine all ingredients in blender. Puree until smooth. Add water or non-dairy milk to thin shake if consistency is too thick.

Minty Cucumber & Apple Smoothie

This is a very fresh tasting smoothie, and the mint adds a nice touch!

Serves 1

Ingredients

1 apple
1 cucumber
1 cup water
¼ cup chopped fresh mint leaves
2 Tbsp. agave nectar
1 Tbsp. fresh lemon juice
A few ice cubes

Instructions

Combine all ingredients in blender. Puree until smooth. Add water or non-dairy milk to thin shake if consistency is too thick.

About the Author

Emma Daniels enjoys cooking and eating Vegan! You can usually find her doing just that or reading books – both of which are her favorite pastimes!

Other Books by Emma:

Quick & Easy Vegan Recipes: The No-Hassle, Quick & Easy Vegan Recipes Cookbook of Plant Based, Delicious Meals!

Vegan Slow Cooker: The Set & Forget Vegan Slow Cooker Cookbook of Plant Based, Delicious Meals!

Made in the USA
Las Vegas, NV
22 July 2022

52046753R00042